1

ACKNOWLEDGMENTS

The author wishes to express his gratitude to the following people for the advice, information, and assistance they so willingly gave during the past ten years of publication.

Ward Noxon & Sally Noxon . . . . Skin Diving Hawaii

Ken Taylor . . . . South Sea Aquatics

Pat Wolter . . . . Commercial Diver

Andy Jones . . . . McWayne Marine Supply, Ltd.

Duke King . . . . Professional Diver

Fred Uggla . . . . Underwater Photographer

Jack Ackerman . . . . Professional Diver

Kenji Ego . . . . Division of Fish and Game

Tookie Evans . . . . Kuilima Hotel

Fourth Printing 1973

THE COVER

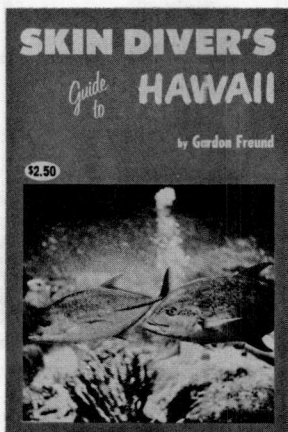

The Island of Maui, lying in the center portion of the main chain of the Islands of Hawaii, has long been noted for the beauty of its coral and the clarity of its water. The two ulua shown with the diver are among Hawaii's most prized game fish.

The photograph was taken by one of Hawaii's most noted underwater photographers Fred Uggla at a depth of 40 feet.

TABLE OF CONTENTS

THE AUTHOR

GORDON FREUND

Since his arrival in the Islands in 1952, Mr. Freund has been prominent in water sports. His interest in diving dates back to 1949 when he began scuba diving off the shores of Malibu, California. During the ensuing years he has spent countless hours beneath the sea gathering information as a writer and pursuing the sport of spearfishing.

For the past five years, Mr. Freund has been the water sports columnist for the *Honolulu Star-Bulletin*. His assignments have taken him to diving areas throughout the island chain; and, most recently, to Tahiti in the South Pacific.

Skin Diver's Guide to Hawaii is Mr. Freund's third diving book. His first, Skindiving Guide to Hawaii, was published in 1958 and was an immediate success. In addition, Mr. Freund has written many feature articles for both newspapers and magazines.

PHOTOGRAPHY

RON CHURCH

Ron Church's prowess as a submarine photographer has become firmly established through his many underwater photographs published in national magazines and books such as: Time, Life, Scientific American, Holiday, Fathom and Skin Diver. Since his entry into the field of professional photography 12 years ago his picture assignments have carried him from heights of 50,000 feet at speeds of Mach 2, shooting aerial photographs for Convair Aircraft Corp., to 200 foot depths beneath the ocean to photograph black coral.

As a skin diver since the age of 16, he has held 3 world spearfishing records, one being a 464 lb. black sea bass. He is a member of the famed San Diego "Addicts" skin diving club.

All photographs not otherwise credited in this book have been taken by him.

INTRODUCTION

Few areas of the world offer more ideal diving conditions than the islands of Hawaii. Their mildly tropical climate and warm clear sea invite enthusiasts the year round.

Extending from the jagged cliffs of the Pali Coast on Kauai to South Point on the island of Hawaii, the major islands of the Hawaiian Archipelago are readily accessible to all; most by means of a highly modern air network, the others by sea. On the individual islands there is an extensive system of highways and superior accommodations which have made even their most remote areas available. In addition to these factors, the waters of Hawaii contain some of the most colorful and gamelike fish to be found. Considering all this makes it easy to understand why Hawaii has attracted more diving enthusiasts per capita than most areas of the world.

Nearly forty years ago a small group of Hawaiian men, including the famed Duke Kahanamoku, crudely fashioned small, glass bottomed boxes and long hardwood poles with barbless steel tips. Swimming along the surface of the water they could look down on the coraled bottom; and, with a jabbing motion, impale the fish. Then, forcing the pole tightly against the reef floor, they swam down its length to retrieve their quarry. A few years after this rude beginning, goggles of hand carved bamboo were imported from the Orient; and the simple pole spear was replaced with what is widely known as the Hawaiian Sling. The men became even more proficient and the popularity of the sport grew. Today, with the advent of a vast amount of highly specialized equipment, diving has become appealing to people from all walks of life. This is especially true of Hawaii where the visitor and resident alike may so easily exeprience the beauty of the tropical sea.

For the more experienced diver, Hawaii's deeper offshore waters remain relatively unexplored; and the fighting quality and size of its game fish are second to none.

Moorish Idols in shallow reef waters off Kailua, Kona.

THE FISH OF HAWAII

The fish discussed in this section are those species with which the diver will be primarily concerned. Of the 600 odd variety of fish found in Hawaiian waters, only a comparative handful are of value as either a source of food or game with respect to spear-fishing. They are not generally limited to any specific area; however there are areas in which certain species do appear in greater abundance, and it is practical to consider their population as being consistent throughout the island chain. Being familiar with the general habits and types of areas in which individual fish are found is invaluable with respect to diving expediency and efficiency. For a more positive identification, the Hawaiian common and scientific name of each fish will be given.

REEF FISH

Although some species of reef fish will be found to depths as great as 150 or 160 feet, they are generally confined to the shallow inshore areas of the reef itself.

AAWA
Wrasse *(Bodianus bilunulatus)*

> The aawa is one of the few roamers of the reef fish family, often seen among but not part of the general group. As a food source it is only fair. They rarely exceed 4 or 5 pounds; and, as is common with most members of the wrasse family, are frequently seen free swimming. Predominent colors are yellow, black, and white.

AHOLEHOLE
Mountain Bass *(Kuhlia sandvicensis)*

> One of the noturnal feeding species whose large eyes are light sensitive. During the day it is most often found in schools within the coral caverns. It seldom exceeds 6 or 7 inches in length, and is an excellent food fish. Color, bright silver.

ALAIHI
Indian Fish *(Holocentrus spinifer)*

One of the most deep and compressed bodied of all the Hawaiian Squirrel-fish Family. It has the large eyes of nocturnal fish, and is usually seen singly. It is an extremely curious fish. Divers spearing within ledges are often surprised by its bold approach, as it seemingly appears out of nowhere from the darkened recesses. They commonly run from 3 to 5 pounds, but specimens up to 7 pounds have been speared. In addition to their bright red color, they are further distinguished by a long sharp barb on the gill plate which can inflict a nasty wound. They are a fair food source; and as with other fish of their coloring, are referred to with the collective term . . . RED FISH.

After spearing an Aweoweo, Rick Grigg notices a Tiger Cowry lying on a coral ledge.

AWEOWEO
Big Eye *(Priacanthus cruentatus)*

Another of the nocturnal feeders that spends most of the daylight hours hidden within the coral caverns. When danger approaches, they will often lie in a recess scarcely larger than their own body, depending on their coloration to hide them. They average 6 to 8 inches in length and are sometimes found in schools. Their color is variable, ranging from red to mottled red and silver. They are a good food source.

HUMUHUMU-NUKUNUKU-A-PUA'A
Trigger Fish *(Rhinecanthus rectangulus)*

Although its name has been made famous in the songs of Hawaii, the "humu" is actually a rather innocuous looking fish. It has a set of human-like teeth which are capable of giving the careless diver a painful bite. When pursued, they retreat into small holes in the coral and securely wedge themselves by erecting their large, trigger-like dorsal spine. To extract them from the holes, it is necessary to reach in and lower the trigger. When molested they will often make a clearly audible grunting noise. Though they are not sought as a food source, they do make attractive aquarium specimens. Average length is about 6 inches, and their color is a composite of black, yellow, and red.

KALA
Unicorn Fish *(Naso unicornis)*
One of the oddest looking and most resourceful of the reef fish group. When pursued by divers, it will often gain entry to small openings in the coral by turning its body sideways or lie flat against the roof of a coral cavern. Unless a diver is familiar with these techniques, the fish may be overlooked. 3 to 5 pounds sizes are common. They are as lacking in color, a dull grey-green, as they are in edibility.

KUMU
Goat Fish *(Parupeneus porphyreus)*
Easily distinguished by their overall red coloring, catfish like feelers, and a white saddle near the tail; the kumu is one of the finest eating fish to be found in Hawaiian waters. They are quite often seen swimming slowly in and out of coral ledges near sandy bottomed areas, usually in schools. Although most that have been speared range in the 1 to 3 pound class, individual specimens from 6 to 9 pounds have been reported.

Diver Charles Lewis prepares to spear a kumu in the waters off Moku Manu.
—Jimmy Smith photo

10

LION FISH
Fire Fish *(Pterois sphex)*

One of the most beautiful yet dreaded of Hawaiian fish. It has poisonous spines which can inflict extremely painful, though seldom lethal, wounds. Its favorite habitate is on the roofs or sides of coral caverns. During the evening hours it often comes out in the open in search of food.

Because of their scarcity, and the perfection with which they blend into their surroundings, it is not commonly seen by divers. Sometimes its elongated fins are mistaken for the antenae of the banded coral shrimp which usually shares coral caverns with it. Coloration is generally a reddish brown with yellowish white stripes or bands. Though not speared divers should be cognizant of its presence. The common size is around 6 inches.

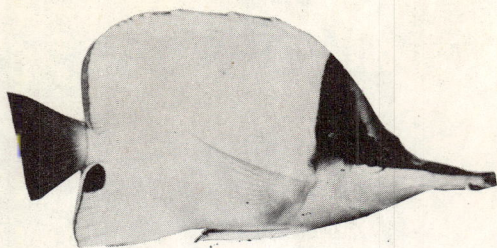

LAU WILIWILI

Long Nosed Butterfly Fish *(Forcipiger longirostris)*

Although it has the typically striking coloration of most members of the butterfly fish family; the elongated mouth, with which it probes into tiny recesses for food, makes the "long nose" worthy of mention. They are commonly seen swimming upside down in caves or other areas, where they seem to have completely lost their relationship with the bottom. They are yellow and black in color and reach a length of about 6 inches. They are not sought for food; but, like most butterfly fish, make excellent aquarium specimens.

MU

Porgie *(Monotaxis grandoculis)*

Human-like molar teeth and a shyness that most often frustrates divers makes the mu one of the most unusual of Hawaiian fish. Frequenting the deeper portions of the reef area, they are slow moving free swimmers that seemingly prefer to stay just beyond spearing range. Red lips and a silver body with dark bands make them easy to recognize. Three to 6 pound sizes are common, but they may get as large as 8 or 9 pounds. They are considered a good food source.

MENINI

Convict Tang *(Acanthurus sandvicensis)*

Common to the more shallow waters of the reef, the menini is easily distinguished by its bright yellow body with black verticle stripes. As with all surgeon fish, they have a small bone-like projection at the base of their tail and should be handled with care. They are often seen swimming around coral heads and ledges, sometimes singularly but more commonly in schools. Seldom exceeding 5 to 6 inches, they are considered a good food fish.

Large school of Kumu feeding off the shallow reefs of Waikiki

NENUE
Chub *(Erythroclus schlegelii)*

Unlike most reef fish. the nenue is often a mid-water swimmer. They are frequently seen in schools moving actively amist the aerated water of the shore break. When pursued, they will often gather in groups within a coral cave; and they become easy prey to divers. They range from light silver to dark grey in color and average 4 to 6 pounds in weight. A few 10 to 12 pounders have been speared with some reports running as high as 16. They are excellent fighters, but they are lacking in food quality. Many divers believe they readily attract shark when speared.

13

NOHU
Scorpion Fish (Scorpaenopsis cacopsis)

Because of its masterful natural camouflage; the nohu is very often overlooked by divers, even when they are within close proximity. As is characteristic of members of the scorpion fish family, they have large heads and mouths. Their corsal spines contain a mild poison which can cause a painful wound to the diver unfortunate enough to be wounded by them. They the usually found lying on the sandy bottom or in coral caves waiting for some unsuspecting prey to come close enough for them to make short lunge to devour it. They are considered a delicacy and average 4 to 6 pounds in size. Color is usually a reddish brown with red pectoral cavities.

PALANI
Surgeon Fish (Acanthurus dussumieri)

So named because of the two scalpel-like barbs contained at the base of its tail, the surgeon fish or palani quickly gains the respect of the divers who handle it. Carelessness in handling it, or an attempt to grab it by its tail section, can result in a severe wound. A usual member of any reef fish group, it will quickly turn to the protection of the coral when molested. Although there are several species, most are a dark purple. Large specimens may measure up to 18 inches. They are a poor food source.

Jerry Frost observes surgeon fish swimming lazily over the coral.

14

UHU
Parrot Fish *(Scarus perspicillatus)*
Named for the parrot-like beak they use in breaking and chewing coral; the uhu is commonly seen by divers as it wanders over wide areas of the reef. It is one of the largest and most colorful members of the inshore family. Although they have been seen at depths in excess of 200 feet, the majority of them remain within shallow water. When sleeping or hiding in the coral, they often change their coloring to suit the surroundings. Divers learn to spot them by looking for their predominantly white beak or large eye. Color varies but most are either a reddish-brown or a brilliant blue. Many 8 to 14 pounders have been speared, but they generally run smaller. They are a good food fish.

Charles Smith retrieves a large uhu speared in the recesses of a coral ledge.
Note the 3 prong spear.

15

U'U
Menpachi *(Myripristis argyromus)*

Probably no other fish is so widely sought as this member of the red fish group. Like its cousin, the aweoweo, it feeds nocturnally and spends most of the day hidden within the coral caves and ledges, often in small schools. When approached they emit a grunting noise, darting swiftly between the extremities of their coral recess. Its excellence as a food fish is attested by its wide popularity with island people. Characteristic of members of the squirrelfish family, it has large eyes and a dark red body. Average size is 6 to 8 inches.

Jack Ackerman, Pete Wilson, and Wally Young with 4 spears of Menpachi taken off Koko Head—Wally Young photo.

WEKE
Goat Fish *(Mulloidichthys samoensis)*

A knowledge of the weke is important to divers who wish to spear large game fish; as several species, especially the ulua and kahala, feed heavily upon them. At depths of 60 to 100 feet they are often found in schools nearing $\frac{1}{2}$ ton, swimming closely together in a large circular pattern near the bottom upon which they feed. Typical of the goat fish family, they have long whisker-like barbles with which they grub in the sand in search of food. Near shore they are usually smaller in number and size. Sizes vary between 8 and 12 inches as a rule, and they are more often sought with a net than a spear. There are both red and white varieties. An excellent food source.

Gordon Freund shown with record 67 ½ pound Kahala he speared at Waikiki's famous "100 foot hole".

GAME FISH

As with the reef fish group, the game fish of Hawaii cannot properly be classified as inhabiting one particular area, namely the deeper offshore waters. Actually there is a general overlapping of the areas in which both groups are generally found. But divers do seek and find the greatest number of game fish in the deeper offshore waters.

KAKU
Barracuda *(Sphyraena barracuda)*

Seldom seen or speared in Hawaiian waters, it is indeed a rare catch. Curious but extremely wary, they are difficult fish for divers to approach. Though the largest reported catch was 80 pounds, specimens nearing 6 feet are frequently brought in by commercial fishermen. Young barracuda are commonly seen in the lagoons and harbors of the islands. Silver and black in color, they are a fine food fish.

KAHALA
Amberjack *(Seriola dumerilii)*

Most divers agree that the kahala is a deep water fish, occasionally seen on the outer fringes of the reef but most frequently at depths of 60 to 100 feet. Typical of the jack family, they are free swimming roamers that are often seen in pairs feeding on weke schools. Sizes range to well over 100 pounds with the average being between 30 and 40. In the water they appear silver with a pronounced yellow stripe running horizontally along the spine. They seem to have a curious nature, and will often approach a diver from open water. The present State record of 82 pounds was speared by Bill Anderson in 90 feet of water off Waikiki. They are superb fighters and a fine food fish.

19

ULUA
Jack Crevalle *(Carangoides ajax)*

The ulua is the most sought after game fish by divers in Hawaii. It ranges from the shallow waters of the reef to depths of 600 feet. There are several species with varying habits, but basically it is a free swimmer that often seeks the protection of coral ledges and caves. Difficult to classify, it is seen singly, in pairs, and large schools. Like kahala, it preys on weke schools. Experienced divers seek ulua in the grottos and deep ledges of the lava coastline, or in areas where the bottom drops off sharply. They range from a few pounds to an estimated 200. The present world record (with a Hawaiian sling) is 127 pounds. It was speared off the Waianae coast in 40 feet of water by Jack Ackerman. The ulua has few equals as a fighter and is a favorite food fish throughout the islands. Among the several species color runs from silver to near black.

Jack Ackerman and his world record 127 pound ulua. It was speared with a single shot from a Hawaiian sling in 35 feet of water off Waianae.

After having speared a small ulua, this diver is returning to the surface.

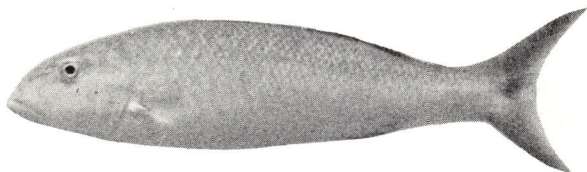

UKU

Grey Snapper *(Aprion virescens)*

The uku is a difficult fish to spear. Unlike the other free swimming fish, it stays well off the bottom and is extremely wary. They are most frequently seen swimming slowly in the distance in the deeper offshore waters. The average size is 4 to 8 pounds, although some specimens run as high as 30 or 40. It is a good food source and an excellent fighter.

Larry Windley proudly displays the 354 pound sea bass he speared in 110 feet of water off Lahaina, Maui.

HAWAIIAN SEA BASS
Grouper *(Epinephelus tauvina)*

This large grouper is a rarity in Hawaiian waters. During the past decade, only a handful of sightings and catches have been reported. Most were seen in or near large caves at depths ranging from 40 to 200 feet. Size ranges from a few to an estimated 10 or 12 feet, with weights of at least 800 pounds. One specimen caught by hand line in the harbor at Nawiliwili on the island of Kauai neared the 800 pound mark. The present State record for spearing is 410 pounds. It was caught in 90 feet of water in a cave off the Windward Coast. The two divers who share credit for the catch used Hawaiian slings.

SHARKS · RAYS · OCTOPUS

SHARK

It is widely agreed that sharks are not overly abundant in Hawaiian waters, especially in the shallow reef areas. They are more apt to be seen by SCUBA divers working in depths of 40 to 100 feet than by skin divers close to shore. Generally their interest in the diver is no more than casual. However, when speared fish are left lying on the bottom unattended; a diver stands a good chance of losing them. Size usually varies between 4 and 8 feet, or occasionally larger. There are many varieties, but sand, tiger, and hammerheads are most common.

Gray Shark, commonly called a Black Tip Shark. Note dark spots on tips of fins. An ulua swims in the background.

Leapord Ray cruising in the Makapu, Rabbit Island area.

Photo by Bert Lang

Manta Ray in the Kona area. There were two of them and this one has a spread of approximately 25 feet. (1971)

Photo by Bert Lang

RAYS

Like sharks, rays are infrequently seen in Hawaiian waters and seem to prefer the outer reef and deeper water areas. The gray and spotted sting rays are the ones most commonly seen, usually lying in the sand bottomed channels that interlace the coral. Several sting rays in the 200 pound class have been speared, though they are estimated to run as high as 400 pounds. Occasionally large manta rays are seen from shore or reported by divers.

OCTOPUS

The octopus, or squid as it is widely referred to locally, is a food favorite among island people. It is found abundantly in both the reef and offshore waters, usually from 1 to 4 pounds in size. Much of its time is spent hidden in small holes within the coral. An ability to change its coloring to blend perfectly with its surroundings and a trick of piling small stones to hide the entrance of its hole, places it among the most difficult forms of marine life for inexperienced divers to spear.

Jim Froman points to a large octopus that seems to have a permanent grip on his hand. However, it soon ended in his diving bag.

LOBSTER · TURTLE

LOBSTER

As do most of the RED FISH, lobster feed nocturnally and remain hidden in the holes and ledges of the coral during the day. They range from the shallow waters of the reef to depths of around 125 feet. By most standards Hawaiian lobster are small, averaging 2 to 4 pounds; but some 7 to 9 pounders have been taken. They are an excellent food source.

A curious lobster cautiously departs from his cavern.

Nearly exhausted, diver Neil Tobin rests on the beach after having fought this turtle a quarter of a mile to shore off Naniloa.

TURTLE

Two kinds of turtle frequent Hawaiian waters, the Hawk's Bill and the Green Sea Turtle. Of the two the Hawk's Bill is smaller, 20 to 80 pounds, and is highly prized for its beautiful shell. The Green Sea Turtles run well into the 300 to 400 pound class, and are mostly sought as a food source. Divers often find them sleeping on sand bottomed caves; and, if they are not too large, try and take them by hand. Otherwise, they are speared through the neck or front flipper. They apparently prefer the outer-reef areas in depths of 40 to 80 feet. They are a fine food source.

27

EEL · VANA · FIRE CORAL

EEL

Hawaii likely has more eels per square foot, yard, or mile than any other area of the world. It is only unusual when one is not found in a coral hole or ledge of any size. They come in a variety of species, most usually the moray. They range from but a foot or two of water to depths over 150 feet, in lengths of at least 6 feet. They rarely make an unprovoked attack, but careless divers have been bitten when placing their hands into unseen areas of the coral. Needle sharp teeth and a powerful jaw make them worthy of every diver's consideration.

Several rows of large sharp teeth make the moray eel king of his domain.
Note vana in the foreground.

VANA

Spiny Sea Urchin

Found throughout the coral crevasses of both the reef and off-shore waters, the vana is one of the most realistic concerns for island divers. When brushed against or stepped on, its needle-like spines will easily penetrate any unprotected part of the body. Though not dangerous, wounds are painful. Black in color, with spines 3 to 4 inches in length, it is easy to recognize.

FIRE CORAL

Contrary to popular opinion, fire coral is a plant-like animal growth found on the more protected portions of rock and coral. Its distribution is irregular throughout most areas of the reef, and it is difficult to see. Though reaction to it varies from individuals, it usually sets up a swelling similar to hives that may last for several days. It is considered more irritating than dangerous.

28

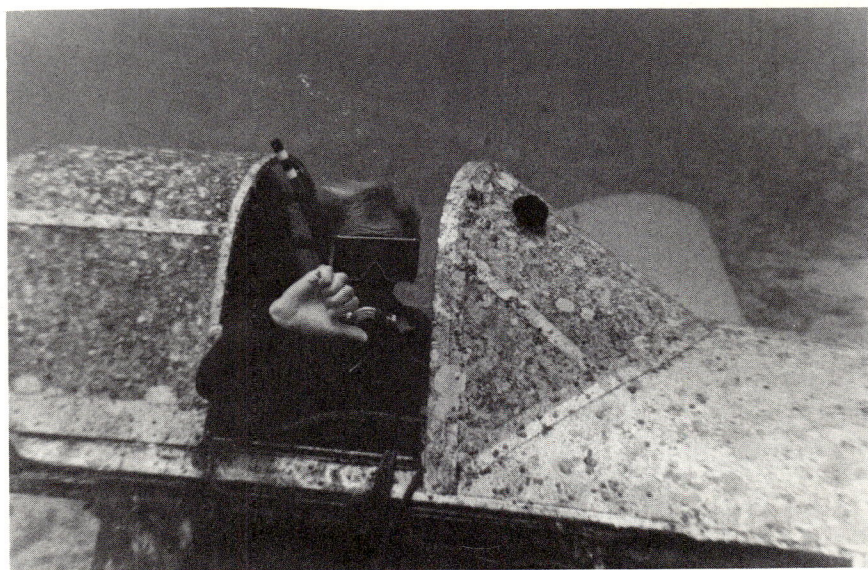

Dave Norquist signals "downed flyer" sitting in the cockpit of a Japanese Zero.

SPEARFISHING

EQUIPMENT AND TECHNIQUE

Considering the amount of diving equipment now available in Hawaii, it is often difficult for the beginning or newly arrived diver to decide what to buy that will best suit the conditions he will encounter in Hawaiian waters. Hawaii does make particular demands on the type of equipment to be chosen, and the following information is given by the authors with the intent that it will be expedient:

EQUIPMENT

MASKS

Although the type of mask you choose will depend largely on the contours of your face, Hawaiian waters are warm and you'll likely be wearing it from a half to several hours; so it should be comfortable.

The gum rubber masks deteriorate more rapidly in a tropical climate, however this doesn't mean you shouldn't pick a mask with a soft skirt; for they are better fitting and also make it easier to equalize the pressure on your ears should you dive below eight or ten feet.

If the mask you select is available with safety glass, it will be a distinct advantage; as most of your diving will be done in and around coral.

FINS

Those that offer full foot coverage will save you from many cuts on the sharp coral. They will also give excellent protection against the ever present vana or spiney sea urchin.

SNORKELS

Since spearing in Hawaiian waters so often requires you to place your head beneath ledges or into coral holes, an all rubber or combination rubber plastic snorkel is preferable as it lessens the chances of its becoming snagged or acting as an obstruction.

SPEARGUNS

Divers in Hawaii have found two types of spearguns to be most practical, the Hawaiian sling and the arbalete. Often, both of these guns are modified to meet specific conditions.

THE ARBALETE

The arbalete is the standard game fish gun of Hawaii. Its power requires that it be used primarily against large free swimming fish; for when used to shoot small reef fish in the coral, a miss is often damaging to the spear. Several important modifications have been made for its use in Hawaiian waters. They are as follows:

SPEAR

The length is often increased to around 5 feet for added penetration. Stainless steel is preferred for its non-corrosive qualities.

BARB

Same as on the Hawaiian sling, but many divers prefer a detachable head as it greatly reduces the chances of a fish tearing itself loose.

LINE

Against large fish, especially ulua over 30 pounds, the standard lines have not held too well; so many divers convert to parachute shroud line.

SHOCK CORD

Often the strongest lines have failed under the initial surge given by a large fish when it is speared. To overcome this, many divers have taken advantage of a system used by commercial fishermen. A heavy length of surgical tubing (about 12 inches) is attached from the head of the gun to the end point of the line. This absorbs the initial shock of the fish's rush and relieves the strain on the line. To date this system has rarely failed.

ACCESSORY ITEMS

The equipment discussed so far is basic to skin diving. Though it is fundamentally sufficient, there are several accessories that will prove invaluable with respect to both safety and convenience.

KNIVES

Most divers have occasion to work with lines while spearfishing, whether it be on a boat or in the water; and a knife is a handy tool to have, especially in the case of possible entanglement. Instances of a knife being used as a defensive weapon are indeed rare in Hawaiian waters, but often divers will use them to aid in killing a fish once it has been speared. There is no kelp in Hawaii and what little seaweed does exist offers no problem to the diver.

FLOATS

The possibility of cramps or exhaustion alone makes some type of flotation gear advisable, but of particular note is the fact that many of the less protected waters of the Islands are subject to occasionally strong currents that may make a return to shore or boat difficult.

PROTECTIVE CLOTHING

The mean annual temperature of the water in Hawaii is 76 degrees, isothermally in most areas to depths nearing 300 feet. By most standards this is quite warm, but after long exposure it may prove chilling. A wet shirt is not only handy from the latter point of view, it will further give protection against cuts and fire coral.

GLOVES

They are essential to diving in tropical waters from several aspects. The sharpness of the coral and vana alone warrant some degree of protection for the hands, but since many species of fish in Hawaii are armed with either tail barbs or needle like dorsal and pectoral fins, the necessary contact with them will be less hazardous with hand coverage.

TABIS

One of the more recent innovations to Island diving is the nylon jikitabi. They are meant to be worn inside the fin and act as protection for the heel when using Rocket Fins. Tabis can be very helpful in getting out over the coral in beach entries while eliminating sand irration between foot and fin. They are also known to prevent rubber reaction experienced by some people.

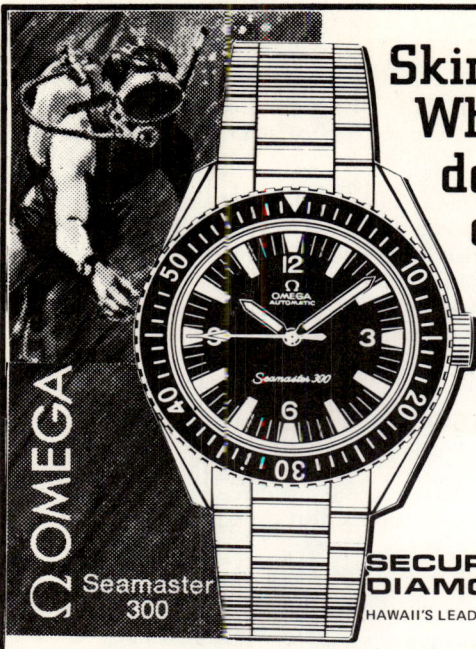

TECHNIQUE

For ease of discussion, technique will be divided into two categories: SKIN DIVING, which will be concerned with the spearing of the smaller fish of the shallow inshore areas; and SCUBA DIVING, which will pertain to the spearing of the larger free swimming fish that normally inhabit deeper waters. It is fully realized that no boundary may actually be placed on these two types of spearing other than for the purpose of discussion, for there is a general overlapping of the two. Technique by shore or boat will be primary to the point of view.

SKIN DIVING

In picking the area in which you wish to dive, it is important to remember that most reef fish are found in rocky or coral bottomed areas that offer them protection against natural enemies. Find these conditions and the chances are good that you will find fish.

If you swim out from shore, it will be wise to pre-select several points of exit, preferably protected sandy areas as an unexpected current may force you to come ashore at a spot other than the one you chose to enter. Having to climb out of the water over a sharp coral reef may bring serious cuts. The distance you fish from shore will be governed by several factors: how rapidly the bottom drops off, the depth at which you are most capable of working, and where you find the fish you want. Hawaii has many areas in which the fringing coral reef will require a diver to swim as much as ¼ of a mile from shore before reaching 20 to 30 foot depths, so it is usually best to have some type of flotation gear along.

When the area you select is readily accessible from shore, it is likely to be often frequented by divers; and the fish will be wary. By whatever means available—boat, inner-tube, raft or just swimming—you will have better results if you can work your way to its remote sections.

Finding fish to spear after you have learned the basic facts is simply a process of swimming along on the surface scouting the possibilities. Many species of reef fish found in Hawaii feed nocturnally, spending the better part of the day hidden in the caverns of the porous coral. Others seen while swimming on the surface will seek immediate refuge in the coral when alarmed; so best results are achieved by diving down to seek them out. With the Hawaiian sling you can reach back into the interior sections of the coral and spear them at close range.

After the first fish is speared you're confronted with the problem of what to do with it. When diving from a boat the solution is simple; otherwise most divers string them to a line attached to a float . . . which may be a coconut, can, bottle or what have you. There near the surface, the fish are seldom bothered by the common predators such as eels or carnivorous fish. Never tie the fish to your waist. This is an exceedingly dangerous habit that might lead to an attack on your person.

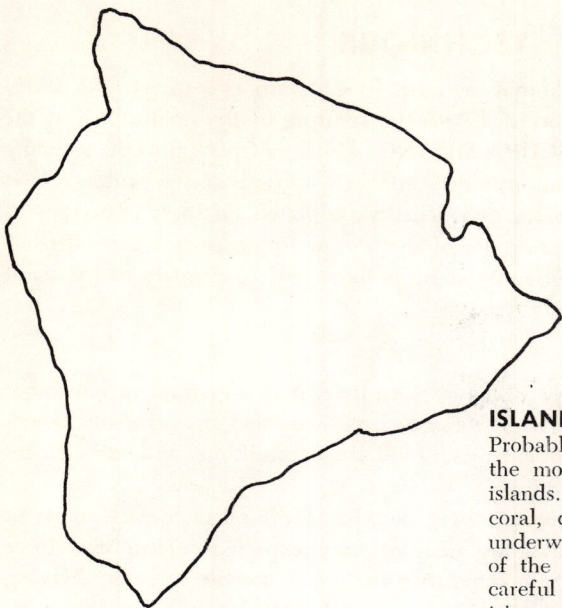

ISLAND OF HAWAII

Probably the island of Hawaii has the most beautiful diving of all the islands. Everything is plentiful; fish, coral, caves and a unique array of underwater lava formations. Because of the rough lava coast line be very careful when making your beach entries and exits. Boat diving is a good way to spend a relaxing day of SCUBA diving, but not necessary in order to find good diving. For the hale and hearty this island has it all.

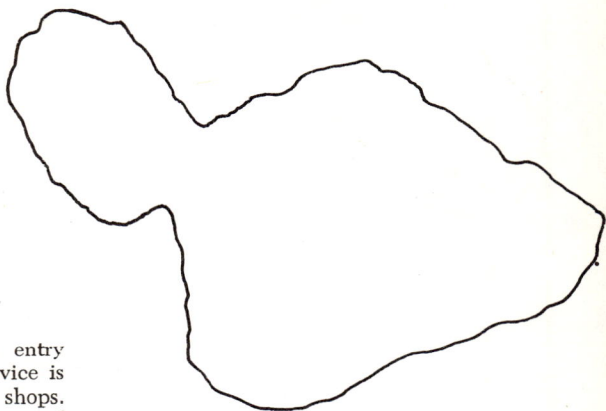

ISLAND OF MAUI

There are many good beach entry areas and also charter boat service is available through most pro dive shops. Don't be afraid to ask the advice of dive shop managers as water conditions tend to change from day to day. Also available from Maui is the Island of Lanai on a full day charter.

ISLAND OF OAHU

SCALE

0 1 2 3 4 5 6 7 8 9 10

MILES

Kawela Bay

K.

Waimea Bay

Kaena Pt.

HALEIWA

MOKULEIA

Yokohama Beach

WAHI

MAKUA

MAKAHA

Pokai
Bay

WAIANAE

WAIPAHU

Nanakuli

EWA

Pearl

Barber's Pt.

LEGEND

⋈	Fish
⬦	Shell
▣	Photography
◗	Approximate Areas at which Trailered Boats may be launched
∿	Main Highway
- - -	Secondary Roads

Kahuku Pt.

IUKU

Laie Pt.

HAUULA

PUNALUU

KAAAWA

WA

Kaneohe Bay
Marina

Moku Manu

KANEOHE

Mokapu Pt.

Kailua

Twin Is.

AIEA

Waimanalo

Rabbit Island

Black Island

Harbor   Sand Is.

HONOLULU

Makapuu Pt.

Waikiki

Portlock

Sandy Beach

Diamond
Head

Black Point

Kokohead

Hanauma Bay

Diver holds Triton's Trumpet shell he has just found at the entrance to Waikiki's "100 foot hole".

SCUBA DIVING

With a lung, you may not only more effectively fish the shallow waters of the reef but the more productive areas beyond it as well. Skin divers in Hawaii seldom spear over 50 or 60 foot depths, and the areas below lie almost completely within SCUBA category.

From shore, lung diving technique is very similar to that of skin diving. If the area is unfamiliar most lung divers prefer to snorkel along the surface, conserving air, until a good area is found. Then, the same searching technique is applied as in skin diving, with the tremendous advantage of having time to more thoroughly probe the less illuminated recesses of the coral.

The benefits of using a lung from shore, as opposed to skin diving, are somewhat over-shadowed by the more limited range of operation. Swimming on the surface with a lung is difficult, and you can only take so much air along. Whenever possible, most island divers prefer to use their lungs from a boat. Here, the technique varies enough to warrant particular consideration. With a boat the lung diver can literally cover miles of territory. Except when going to a specifically known ledge or hole, many divers prefer to conserve their air supply by scouting the general area by one of two methods: looking over the side of the boat through a glass box, or dragging behind the boat at the end of a rope with a mask on. Hawaii's waters are often clear enough to permit viewing to depths of 100 feet; but if the divers wish to see further, they need only to put on their lungs and drag at the 50 or 75 foot level.

By and large it is best to work beyond the range of skin divers when using SCUBA from a boat. There your chances of finding unexplored grounds are good. Many of the species of reef fish, such as the red fish group and uhu or parrot fish, are found in sizeable numbers to depths of 130 or 140 feet. Added to this you will find greater amounts of free swimming game fish like the ulua, kahala, and uku.

The technique of spearing reef fish in deep water is the same as for the reef area, but with the larger free swimming fish it differs greatly. Generally speaking the larger fish, with the frequent exception of the ulua, are not found in the coral ledges and caves. They swim freely in wide areas among the places that offer them food and protection if need be. Unless previously molested by divers their nature is usually curious, often swimming to within a few feet of the diver. With a few species, especially the uku, it is often necessary to arouse their curiosity by remaining partially concealed or with a noise, such as banging on the tank with the butt of your speargun, even throwing up sand from the bottom with your hand. Unlike the reef fish, who remain fairly constantly within a particular area, the free swimmers are more frequently seen in the late afternoon hours. They are definitely easier to spear then as the visibility lessens, and they have to come in closer to investigate anything strange.

While spearing in deeper areas divers often use two guns, a Hawaiian sling for the reef fish and an arbalete for the bigger ones. The arbalete is laid on the coral within a few feet of where the diver is working for use should something big appear. To avoid wasting time, the speared fish are usually stacked on an extra spear; except perhaps for the very large ones, which being harder to kill, are brought directly to the boat.

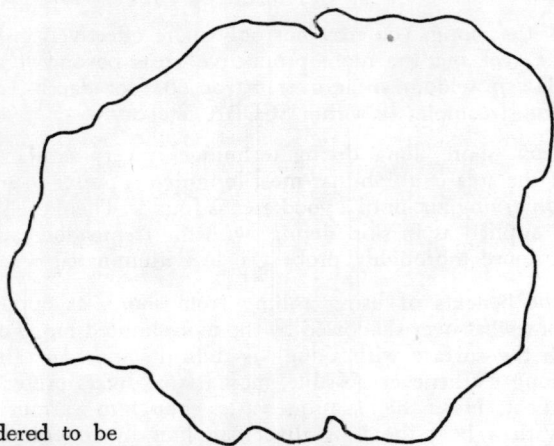

ISLAND OF KAUAI

Diving here is still considered to be excellent for all types of diving. The problems are that no charter service is available and beach entries for SCUBA are few and far between. Snorkeling is abundant and good in almost any area accessible by public road. Please don't go diving during high surf warnings.

SPECIFIC DIVING AREAS

OAHU

There is enough difference between the leeward and windward coasts of the island of Oahu to warrant divers considering them as two distinct areas. In the broadest sense, the seascape of the lee side is flat while that of the windward is irregular with many drops and ledges. In a broad sense it is also true that the waters of the lee side are calm and those of the windward, rough. But these are only partial truths made necessary when attempting to deal comprehensively with so vast an area. Actually the generalizations are realistic, but good and bad conditions do exist in both sections. If the reader will bear these facts in mind, the authors' attempts to evaluate conditions in both areas will be better understood.

THE LEEWARD COAST*

Divers think of the leeward coast as being the area from Kaena Point* to Koko Head. Under the conditions of tradewind weather which prevail throughout most of the year, it is the calmer side.

WAIANAE

From Kaena Point south to Makaha the bottom is fairly well broken-up and spearing is considered to be good. Though all types of fish exist, the area is best noted for menpachi, kumu, and occasionally large ulua. Past Makaha to the southern extreme of Nanakuli the bottom generally flattens out, and the spearing becomes more sketchy.

BARBER'S POINT

Due to the usually dirty water and choppy seas, this area is but occasionally worked by divers. Under favorable conditions, it is very productive as there are many ledges and caves. Accessibility is normally by boat.

*See map page ??

PEARL HARBOR

Like Barber's Point the water here is often dirty. Because of military restrictions, spearing is contained to the outer sections of the channel. It is a productive area with respect to menpachi, kumu, and lobster.

SAND ISLAND

Spearing in this area is but average, and the water here is also frequently dirty. On the inshore portion there are a number of deep coral canyons in which turtle are commonly seen. Beyond the reef the area becomes generally flat.

WAIKIKI (See Special Section, Page 42)

BLACK POINT

This area, like Waikiki and Hanauma Bay, is especially good for beginning divers. There is a rather sharp drop at the breaker-line, and spearing along this ledge is fairly good. At the 30 and 40 foot levels some exceptionally large kumu are speared.

PORTLOCK

The inshore portion of the bay here is dirty, and a boat is required to get to the remote area of the outer reef. At this point there are some sizeable ledges along which spearing is fairly good.

WAIKIKI

Probably no othr area in the islands is dived so much as Waikiki. Lying in the protection of Diamond Head with relatively calm and fairly clean water, it is an excellent area for beginners. Inshore the bottom tapers off very gradually until the outer reef or breaker line with an average depth of 6 to 10 feet. It is generally flat with occasional sand channels, small coral heads, and ledges.

Though generally thought of as having been fished out, there is still a large variety of small reef fish for the novice to spear, photograph, or view. Species consist mostly of uhu, palani, kala, menini, menpachi, kumu, and aweoweo. Though not plentiful, lobster are scattered throughout the area. Beyond the reef, the bottom drops off more rapidly; and, though still generally flat, there are some spectacular sand channels of unusual width and depth. Spearing is sparse; but in areas where weke are found, some noteworthy game fish have been taken. Species other than those included for the inshore area are: ulua, kahala, uku, and sting rays.

Access to the inshore area may be made anywhere along the beach. Preferred grounds lie directly offshore from: the Elks Club, Fort De Russy, and the Hawaiian Village Hotel. The area beyond the reef should be dived from a boat.

THE WINDWARD COAST*

The Windward Coast is prevailingly buffeted by winds from the open sea, with resulting choppy to rough waters. Its bottom and shore are rugged with excellent spearing throughout most areas. During periods of south or light variable winds the waters calm and diving conditions become ideal.

HANAUMA BAY

Well protected inner waters make this a choice location for beginners. As in most of the Windward areas, the water here is normally clean. At the outer portions of the bay, depth ranges from 60 to 80 feet; and there are many fish.

SANDY BEACH

This area has long been known as one of the finest parrot fish grounds in the islands. It is especially convenient for skin divers, as fish are found close to shore in rather shallow water. At times the current here becomes quite strong, and divers should be cautious.

MAKAPUU—RABBIT ISLAND

Beginners as well as experienced divers find this an excellent diving area. The inshore section is sandy and produces many fine helmet shells. The area around the island is well broken-up with some large drops at which many big ulua have been speared.

*See map pages 36-37

WAIMANALO BAY

Best results are had in this often flat area if divers do extensive scouting. In spite of the general flatness, there are occasional ledges and crevasses in which fish are plentiful.

KANEOHE—MOKU MANU

The bottom of the bay is consistently flat, but what few ledges are to be found do produce some outstanding red fish spearing. As with Waimanalo, a good deal of scouting is necessary. Toward and around the island of Moku Manu the bottom becomes broken-up with splendid ledges and caves. Spearing here is very good, and many large game fish are taken.

HAUULA—LAIE POINT

This is one of the most prominent red fish and lobster grounds to be found in the islands. It is well broken-up with several spectacular ledges and cliffs, especially near the point. Kumu and lobster are particularly large. Ulua are frequently seen here, as well as turtles.

KAHUKU

The waters of this area are so continually rough that it has remained one of the few nearly virgin grounds of Oahu. Its bottom is broken, and there are many deep ledges. Spearing of all types is very outstanding.

HALEIWA—MOKULEIA

Spearing along this broad area is excellent. The bottom is very rugged, and all types of fish are plentiful. The water is most calm during the summer months, and most sections are readily accessible from shore. Toward Kaena Point the currents become noticeably stronger, and divers should exercise care, especially in the offshore regions.

STATE OF HAWAII

HANALEI

Kauai

NAWILIWILI

WAIMEA

PORT ALLEN

SHADING INDICATES KNOWN AREAS
FREQUENTED BY DIVERS

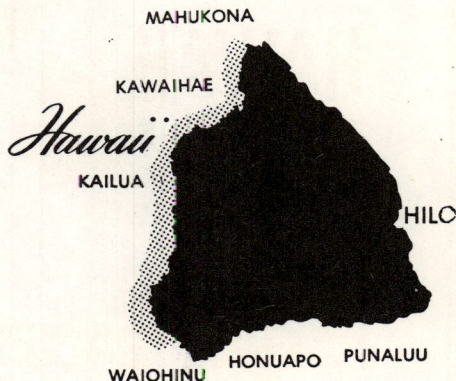

WAIALUA

HALEIWA

Oahu

KANEOHE BAY

PEARL HARBOR

HONOLULU

DIAMOND HEAD

Molokai

KAUNAKAKAI

LAHAINA

KAUMALAPAU

WAILUKU

KAHULUI

Lanai LANAI CITY

Maui

MAHUKONA

KAWAIHAE

Hawaii

KAILUA

HILO

HONUAPO PUNALUU

WAIOHINU

ISLAND OF MOLOKAI

There is no dive shop on this island but there is a compressor, owned by Junior Rawlins. To contact Jr., who often-times is out diving in these turtle-rich waters, contact his brother Larry at the Chevron Station in Kaunakakai. Best bet on this island is a boat dive, weather permitting, to the fabulous North Shore.

44

Dallas Bradford and Ed Scheafer, armed with underwater cameras, peer cautiously into a cave, hoping not to disturb the fish they wish to photograph.

UNDERWATER PHOTOGRAPHY
and
PHOTOGRAPHERS

With a nearly year round clarity and an abundance of colorful fish, the waters of Hawaii provide one of the finest locations in the world for underwater photography. With a little practice, even the beginning photographer can get good results. Although conditions may vary from area to area, most locations will afford enough visibility to assure good underwater pictures.

Because there is less plankton and algae in the waters of Hawaii as compared to the Mainland, it is necessary to adjust the iris of your camera to match the increased amount of light. A list of recommended starting exposures for various films is listed on page 50 These are only for average conditions and may have to be deviated from after shooting a few rolls.

UNDERWATER PHOTOGRAPHERS

Ken Taylor
South Seas Aquatics
at McWaynes
Ph. 538-7724

Ward Noxon
Skin Diving Hawaii
1651 Ala Moana
Ph. 941-0548

Pat Wolter
American Divers
Ph. 536-3121

Photo Courtesy of Skin Diving Hawaii, Inc.

UNDERWATER CAMERAS

Wholesale:

SEACOR

NIKONOS

McWayne Marine Supply, Ltd.
1125 Ala Moana Blvd.
Honolulu, Hawaii
Phone 521-3411

Retail:

Skin Diving Hawaii
1651 Ala Moana Blvd.
Phone 941-0548

Lahaina, Maui
Phone 368-833

P.O. Box 2064
Kailua-Kona
Phone 329-3977

South Seas Aquatics
at McWaynes
1125 Ala Moana Blvd.
Phone 538-7724

Hawaii Camera Co.
1106 Union St.
Phone 536-8173

1415 Kapiolani Blvd.
Phone 949-5321

235 Keawe Street
Hilo, Hawaii
Phone 935-8337

Hawaiian Divers
P.O. Box 572
Kailua-Kona
Phone 329-3407

Rental:

Skin Diving Hawaii
1651 Ala Moana Blvd.
Phone 941-0548

Lahaina, Maui
Phone 368-833

P.O. Box 2064
Kailua-Kona
Phone 329-3977

South Seas Aquatics
at McWaynes
1125 Ala Moana Blvd.
Phone 538-7724

Hawaii Camera Co.
1106 Union St.
Phone 536-8173

1415 Kapiolani Blvd.
Phone 949-5321

235 Keawe Street
Hilo, Hawaii
Phone 935-8337

Hawaiian Divers
P.O. Box 572
Kailua-Kona
Phone 329-3407

*See map pages 36-37

AVERAGE EXPOSURE CHART

SIMPLE CAMERAS: Nikonos, Konica, etc.

Film	asa	depth
Black and White		

Plus X	160	Shallow water
Tri X	400	Deep water

Color

Ektachrome	32	Shallow water
Anscochrome	32	Shallow water
Kodacolor	32	Shallow water
Ektachrome SO 270	160	Deep water
Super Anscochrome	100	Deep water

ADJUSTABLE CAMERAS

Film	asa	depth	exposure

Black and White

Plus X Pan	160	0-50'	100 @ F11
		50-100'	100 @ F8
Tri X Pan	400	0-50'	(not recommended)
		50-100'	100 @ F22
		100-150'	100 @ F8-11

Color

* Ektachrome (reg.)	32	0-50'	100 @ F4.5
		50-100'	100 @ F3.5
* Ektachrome Professional	45-60	0-50'	100 @ F7
		50-100'	100 @ F5.6
		100-150'	100 @ F4.5
* Anscochrome (reg.) . . . Eee Ektachrome reg. . . .			
Super Anscochrome	100	0-50'	100 @ F11
		50-100'	100 @ F8
		100-150'	100 @ F5.6

* In some cases the use of a blue flash bulb will fill in the foreground shadows giving a more pleasing picture.

Jeanie Curren surfaces with a menpachi she speared while skindiving off Makaha.
—Bev Morgan photo

HAWAIIAN SHELLS

Hawaii is one of the most prolific shell areas of the world. There are over 1500 varieties to be found in its waters. Of these, many are endemic or larger in size than other like specimens. From the diver's point of view, which is frequently that of a novice, shells are broadly classified into five categories. They are: Cone, Cowry, Helmet, Triton, and Auger. They may be found from the very shallow reef waters to the depth of the diver's physical limitations. The greatest percentage of shells are found beneath dead and live coral heads. It is usually necessary to use special equipment in collecting them. Most often this will include a pair of gloves to prevent cuts in handling the coral, a crow bar to overturn the heads, and a shell bag for specimens (an old sock works well for this purpose). It is important for collectors to practice conservation while hunting for shells. Unless the overturned coral heads are returned to their original position, the eggs of unhatched shells and other marine animals are apt to die from exposure.

Shirley Church, the co-author's wife, finds a large Tiger Cowry while skin diving off Makua.

AUGERS:

TERIBRA—1. Crenulata, 2. Candida, 3. Chlorata, 4. maculata.

AUGERS

The augers are slender, elongated shells that come to a sharp point at one end. They have a variety of vivid colors and designs which enhance their value. Two good identifying features are their spiral type construction and shiny finish. They are found solely in sandy areas, where they burrow for food like the cones. They also leave a pencil-line trail on the surface of the sand under favorable conditions, and can be found by digging at the small mound at the line's termination.

Some of the augers, such as the Spotted Auger (*Teribra maculata*), attain a size of nearly 9 inches; however, most species are in the 3 to 4 inch class. There are some 200 species distributed in temperate and tropical waters.

COWRIES:

CYPRAEA—1. Chinensis, 2. Tessalatta, 3. Gaskoni, 4. Carneola, 5. Schilderorum, 6. Sulcidentata, 7. Caputseirpentis.

COWRIES

The cowries are likely the most widely sought shells of Hawaii. They have striking color patterns and highly polished surfaces. They are nocturnal animals which seek the protection of coral recesses during the daylight hours. They are most commonly found by overturning coral heads; however, certain varieties seem to prefer the darkness of large caverns. Within the caverns they often crawl back into the small holes of the walls and ceiling.

Certain cowries, such as the Reticulated Cowrie (*Cypraea maculifera*) and the Mauritius Cowrie (*Cypraea mauritiana*) are most commonly found in very shallow waters close to shore. They show a preference for hiding under ledges and in the cracks of the vertical reef faces.

One of the most impressive of all Hawaiian Cowries is the Tiger Cowry (*Cypraea tigris*). Its size is outstanding. Other prized cowries are the Checkered Cowry (*Cypraea tessalatta*) and the Chinese Cowry (*Cypraea chinensis*). There are some 200 species found throughout the world.

CONES

Next to the cowry family, the cones are the most colorful group of shells found in Hawaii. Their name is derived from their conical shape; the narrow end being directed toward the front of the animal. Unlike the cowries, they are found buried beneath the sand as well as in the coral heads. It is sometimes quite easy to find them by following the trail left on the surface of the sand as they burrow along in search of food.

Divers should be aware of the danger in handling the cone shells. Most of them possess poison glands and a dart-like mechanism with which they numb their prey. It is located near the narrow end of the shell, so particular care should be taken to pick them up by the wide or base end.

Though not glossy like the cowries, the cones have many different color patterns and make interesting display pieces. One of the large shell families, there are 500 different species throughout the Pacific.

TRITON—Tritonalia-tritonis

TRITONS

Of the Triton family, the largest and most beautiful is the "Tritons Trumpet" (*Tritonalia tritonis*). Also referred to as the "Horn Shell", they were used by the ancient Polynesians to alert villagers of special events. They were easily made into horns by cutting off about one inch of the pointed ends, and their sounds could be heard for a distance of a quarter mile.

The triton seems to prefer the protection of coral caverns. They are most apt to be seen clinging to the walls or lying on the shelves within. They have a reticulated pattern of white, yellow, and brown with a yellow-orange interior. They attain a length of at least 16 inches.

HELMETS

A large, roughly triangular, heavy shell readily identifies the largest of all Hawaiian molluscs, the Horned Helmet Shell (*Cassis cornuta*). They are found lying partially buried in open sand areas. At first glance they may appear like a small coral growth; but when the series of ridge-like bumps on the dome are recognized, it is easy to tell them apart. The shell is a creamy white on the exterior and orange-brown on the inside. The average size is from 8 to 12 inches. There are several other species of small helmets found in Hawaiian waters, and all of them have the same general characteristics.

CLEANING SHELLS

There are various ways of cleaning shells: They can be boiled, soaked in an alcohol solution, or left to be devoured by insects. However, the preferred method is to freeze them. This way, they can be cleaned at leisure. The common tool used in removing the animal is a hook fashioned of wire. With small shells, a high pressure stream of water will prove effective for parts of the animal that may remain. With some shells, namely the cones and tritons, the exterior is often covered with a calcium growth. This can be removed by immersing them in a chlorox or caustic soda solution. Other growths can be removed with a wire brush.

Shells should not be soaked in fresh water. The deterioration of the animal's flesh may tarnish their finish, this is especially true of the cowries. After shells have been cleaned, it is a good idea to coat them lightly with a silicone compound or vaseline to protect their finish.

The clear water and spectacular coral canyons of Hanauma Bay make it one of the finer locations for underwater photography.

Rick Grigg, hatchet in hand, dislodges a black coral tree from its base in 150 feet of water off Sandy Beach. A school of Opelu Kala swims in the background.

BLACK CORAL

This unique photo of a black coral tree was taken in 190 feet of water.

BLACK CORAL
(Antipathes grandis)

There are over 150 species of black coral found in tropical and sub-tropical waters throughout the world. It inhabits the shallow reef areas to depths estimated as great as 15,000 feet, and it is the largest of all the living corals. The Hawaiian species, *Antipathes grandis,* is indigenous to and found throughout the island chain. Though the *Antipathes grandis* is the only classified Hawaiian species, two others are known to exist. They are referred to by the common names of Pipe and Fern Tree.

The history of Hawaiian black coral dates back to the year 1865 when a group of marine scientists probing the depths off the island of Maui found portions of a "tree" in their dredge. Because of the extreme depth at which is was most predominant and the lack of knowledge concerning its distribution, nearly a century passed before it was to gain prominence.

Several years ago a group of divers descended to a depth of 180 feet off the shores of Lahaina, Maui. Their intent was to explore a legendary site known to local commercial fishermen as the "Stone Wall", a vast, deep water ledge along which game fish were abundant. As they neared the bottom, their eyes fell upon what appeared to be an underwater forest. Curious, they broke one of the "trees" from its foundation; and, at this moment, Hawaii's black coral industry was born.

In its natural setting the black coral tree "roots" itself to a dead coral or rock base. The growth rate is about one foot per year, and individual specimens are known to have reached a spread of 20 feet. Normally, other marine animals such as ascidians, sponges, and oysters, live on the coral trees; and, in association, feed on plankton. The color of the coral comes from its absorption of iodine and varies from a deep, dark brown in a natural state to black when cured.

Today, black coral has become a Hawaiian sea product. Its lustrous ebony finish has placed it in high demand with creative island jewelers. SCUBA divers scour the coastlines of all the islands in a continuing search for new black coral fields.

These are but a few of the outstanding products
into which Black Coral is rendered.

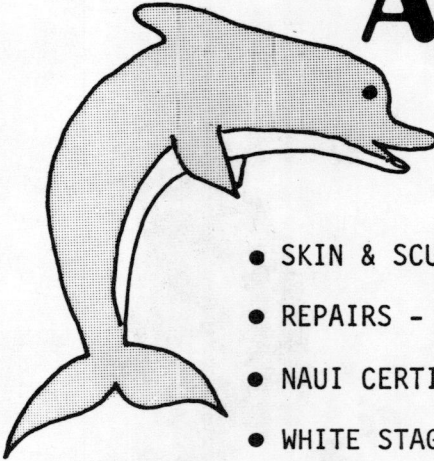

3-lb. uhu shot at 50-ft. depth
off Kailua, Kona
photo by Hawaiian Divers

Diver ascending with a "fern" black coral tree.

OCEANOGRAPHIC RESEARCH
and
SALVAGE

OCEANIC RESEARCH

There are several firms currently doing oceanographic research in Hawaii. Some of their projects will play an important part in the activities of several State agencies. Marine Advisers Inc. has installed a series of wave recording stations at Barber's Point and Kahuku on the island of Oahu, and another at Nawiliwili on Kauai. Transducers, installed by divers at an average depth of 50 feet, give accurate information as to wave heights, frequency, and duration. This information is being used to aid engineers in the designs of harbors, breakwaters, and other waterfront structures subjected to constant wave erosion.

By the end of 1963 a complete marine research center and oceanarium is planned for the Windward side of Oahu. Here, many underwater satellite projects will be carried out. Bio Medical studies are now being undertaken by the International Underwater Associates Company.

SALVAGE AND PROFESSIONAL DIVING

One of the most recent projects utilizing commercial divers was the installation of a submarine pipeline for Hawaiian Independent Refinery by Heally Tibbits Construction Company. The underwater portion of the job was done by American Divers, a Hawaii based diving company.

Other professional diving opportunities are now available in the commercial fishing industry. The use of both scuba and hookah gear is being employed by net fishermen, opening a vast number of hitherto unworkable deep water areas. In the harbors, enterprising divers are making individual contracts that cover anything from the recovery of small articles dropped from the boats to the cleaning and repairing of their bottoms.

In the more highly skilled lines, underwater photography is a field for which there is an ever increasing demand. Few national magazines can afford to overlook prominent diving stories, particularly when accompanies by photographs.

Oceanographers establishing a transducer station to record
wave heights and frequencies.

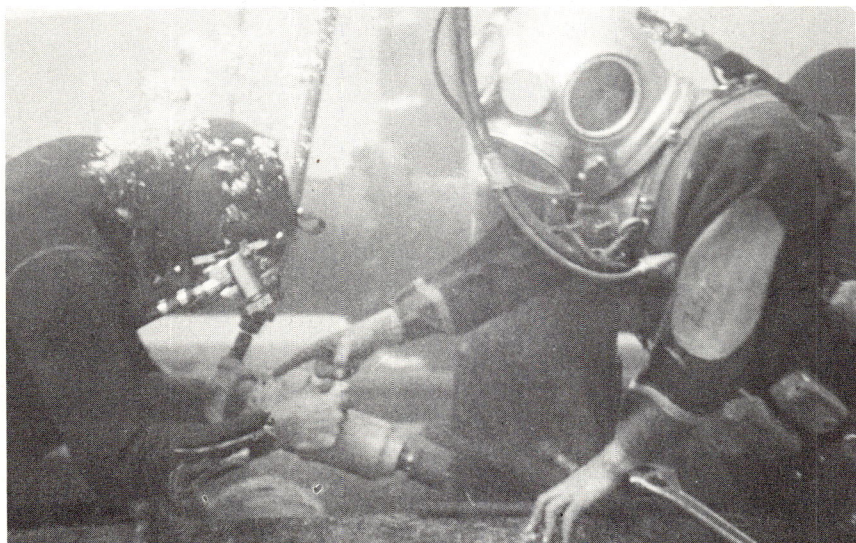

PUBLIC INSTRUCTION

SCUBA

Central Y.M.C.A., 401 Atkinson Dr., Phone 941-3344. For information regarding schedule, costs, and equipment available; it is best to call as classes are subject to change.

Armed Forces Y.M.C.A., 250 So. Hotel St., Phone 536-3735. Classes are open to members of the Armed Forces. Call for information as classes are subject to change. Denis Kirwan, certified instructor.

Black Coral Diving School, N.A.U.I. certification, Honolulu, Phone 536-3121.
Bojac Swim & Scuba School, 94-300 Farrington Hwy., Waipahu, Phone 671-0311.

Pacific Marine Frontiers, Inc., 850 Kam Hwy., Pearl City, Phone 455-1480.
Aarons Outdoor Center, 39 Maluniu Ave., Kailua, Hi.. Phone 261-1211.

Ulua caught in Sandy Beach area by Bert Lang.

Photo by Craig Craw

PRIVATE INSTRUCTION
OAHU

Skindiving—SCUBA

Skin Diving Hawaii, 1651 Ala Moana Blvd., Phone 941-0548. Instruction and charter service with guides. All equipment available.

South Seas Aquatics, or South Seas Aquatics at McWaynes, Phone 538-7724. Instruction and charter service with guides. All equipment available.

MAUI

Skin Diving Hawaii, Lahaina, Phone 368-833. Instruction and charter with complete facilities and air refills provided.

HAWAII

Hawaiian Divers, P. O. Box 572, Kailua-Kona, Hawaii 96740, Phone 329-3407. Instruction and charter service with air refills available.

Skin Diving Hawaii, P. O. Box 2064, Kailua-Kona, Hawaii, Phone 329-3977

At sunset off Waikiik, skin diver Jack Lucas reflects on a day spent beneath the sea.

Beautiful Hanauma Bay on the Windward Shore of Oahu—H.V.B. photo.

DIVING EQUIPMENT
WHOLESALE

Skin Diving Hawaii
Sportsway
1651 Ala Moana Blvd.
Ph. 941-0548

Pacific Sports
Scubapro
845 Halekauwila St.
Ph. 533-2797

McWayne Marine Supply
U.S. Divers
1125 Ala Moana Blvd.
Ph. 521-3411

Clark Sales Inc.
White Stag
P.O. Box 2241
Ph. 677-9135

RETAIL

HONOLULU

Skin Diving Hawaii
1651 Ala Moana Blvd.
Ph. 941-0548

Charley's Fishing Supply, Inc.
745 Keeaumoku Street
Ph. 949-7373

South Seas Aquatics
At McWaynes
1125 Ala Moana Blvd.
Ph. 538-7724

J.C. Penney Co.
Ala Moana
Ph. 946-8086
Pearl Ridge
Ph. 488-0961

OUTER ISLANDS

KAUAI	MAUI	MOLOKAI	HAWAII
Kauai Stores	Skin Diving Hawaii	August Rawlins	Sports Center Hawaii
Lihue	Lahaina, Maui	Kaunakakai	Hilo
	Lahaina Dive Shop		Hawaiian Divers Inc.
	Lahaina, Maui		Kailua, Kona
			Yama's Spec. Shop
			Kailua, Kona

A 12 foot manta ray glides by like a giant bird.

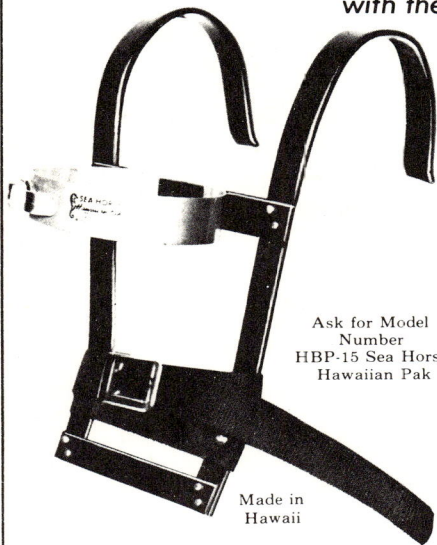

AIR STATIONS
AND EQUIPTMENT SERVICING

OAHU

South Seas Aquatics
(see ad)

Bojac Swim & Scuba
(see ad)

Pacific Marine Frontiers
(see ad)

Dan's Dive Shop

Skin Diving Hawaii, Inc.
(see ad)

Aarons Outdoor Center
(see ad)

Honolulu Sporting Goods

Divers Eqpt. & Services
(see ad)

KAUAI

Kauai Skin Diving Co.
(see ad)

MOLOKAI

August Rawlins Jr.
Kaunakakai

MAUI

Skin Diving Hawaii, Inc.
(see ad)

Lahaina Dive Shop

Salt Water Sportsman
(see ad)

Central Pacific Divers

Kihei Dive Center

HAWAII

Sports Center Hawaii
(see ad)

Skin Diving Hawaii, Inc.
(see ad)

Hawaiian Divers
(see ad)

Aqua-Lung Sales & Service

BOATS AND MOTORS
Retail • Service and Repair

McWayne Marine
Supply Ltd.
  Johnson Motors
Kewalo Basin
Ph. 536-4404

Outboard Sales
& Service
256 Kalihi
Ph. 812-428

Divers investigate sunken WW II Corsair Aircraft in Waianae area.
Photo by Bob Zering

Photographer in action off Maui
photo by Hawaiian Divers

HAWAII COUNCIL OF DIVE CLUBS

Aku Marines	Alii Holo Kai	Bojac
Ph. 254-2487	Ph. 732-1756	Ph. 671-0311
Dive Groupe	Hawaii Divers	Hui Lu'u Kai
Ph. 395-9087	Ph. 941-1383	Ph. 637-9671
Ka Imi Kai	Kai Divers	Na Mea Lu'u Kai
Ph. 373-1434	Ph. 689-0503	Ph. 262-8472
NAIA	Ocean'auts	Pearl Divers
Ph. 624-3892	Ph. 235-5138	Ph. 435-6213
Sea Lancers	Sea Wolves	Tiki Divers
Ph. 422-8646	Ph. 423-1182	Ph. 841-1486

University Aquanauts   Water Rats Dive Club
Ph. 955-3189   Ph. 247-3594

Scuba divers surface with a large catch of reef fish taken off Moku Manu.

Paul Akiona displays the 56 pound ulua
he speared off Mokuleia.

"NO DECOMPRESSION" LIMITS

DEPTH IN-FEET	BOTTOM TIME IN-MIN.	
40	200	**– CAUTION –**
50	100	THIS TABLE GIVES THE MAXIMUM ALLOWABLE BOTTOM TIME (FIGURED
60	60	FROM THE TIME A DIVER
70	50	LEAVES THE SURFACE UNTIL
80	40	HE LEAVES THE
90	30	BOTTOM) THAT PERMITS
100	25	SURFACING DIRECTLY
110	20	AT 60 FOOT PER MINUTE
120	15	WITH NO DECOMPRESSION
130	10	STOPS.
140	10	
150	5	**– CAUTION –**
160	5	THIS TABLE IS GOOD
170	5	FOR ONLY ONE
180	5	DIVE DURING ANY
190	5	12 HOUR PERIOD

COURTESY PACIFIC SPORTS

Divers Larry Smith (standing) Harold Kruger, and John Toomey display the
tub full of fish they speared while diving off Barber's Point.

RECOMPRESSION CHAMBER

The Navy maintains a recompression chamber in the Submarine Base at Pearl Harbor, which in case of emergency may be used by civilian and military personnel alike. The seriousness of the bends cannot be over-emphasized. All SCUBA divers should be familiar with their cause and symptoms. If symptoms should occur, DON'T WAIT, call 422-5955 or 435-6121 immediately.

RULES AND REGULATIONS
STATE OF HAWAII

Division of Fish and Game

Department of Transportation

To date, there have been few regulations passed by the State that specifically restrict the actions of spear fishermen. Rather, they have been guided mainly by the existing laws applicable to sports fishermen. Any actions that may follow will depend largely on the sense of sportsmanship shown by divers with respect to the conservation of marine resources.

The Spearing of the Following Fish is Governed by Length:

SPECIES	INCHES (minimum)
Aholehole — Big Eye	5
Kala — Unicorn fish	9
Kahala — Amberjack	9
Kumu — Goat fish	7
Menini — Convict tang	5
Moana — Goat fish	7
Moi — Thread fish	7
Mullet	7
Opelu Kala	9
Weke — Goat fish	7

The spearing of the Following Fish is Governed by Weight

SPECIES	POUNDS (minimum)
Octopus — (Squid)	1
Uhu — Parrot fish	1
Ulua — Jack crevalle	1
Uku — Grey snapper	1
Lobster	1

LOBSTER

A closed season exists on the procuring of lobster, by any means, from the 1st of June until the 1st of September.

The spearing of lobster is prohibited on all the Islands of Hawaii.

No female lobster may be taken while bearing eggs. (These are carried on the under side of the tail and are made immediately apparent by their vivid orange color.)

NOTE: THE SELLING OF SPEARED FISH IS ILLEGAL THROUGH-OUT THE STATE.

Dacor
the professional's choice

Dacor recognizes the importance of making our products meet the exacting quality standards of men who teach, work and explore the sea. Our long term and consistant commitment to making the finest innovative products has made Dacor *"the professional's choice."*

DACOR

Dacor Corporation
161 Northfield Road
Northfield, Ill. 60093
P.O. Box 157
Cable: DIVECOR